General Knowledge TIMES

SR. VIJAYA C.M.C.

3

GOYAL BROTHERS PRAKASHAN

CONTENTS

Amazing India

Our Wonderful World

Living With Nature

Green and Wild

Exploring Our Surroundings

Health and Happiness

Edition : 2026 Price : ₹ 330

Song
Orphan's
Garden

1 States and Union Territories

There are 28 states and 8 Union Territories in India. Each of these has unique culture and tradition including various languages,dances and festivals.

Quiz Time

1. Choose the wrong pair.
   (a) Rajasthan: Jaipur (b) Tamil Nadu: Chennai
   (c) Ladakh: Leh (d) Mizoram: Kohima
2. I am known for famous pilgrimage sites located in Northern Mountains.
   (a) Haryana (b) Uttarakhand
   (c) Rajasthan (d) Gujarat
3. Which state is famous for the dance Bharatanatyam?
   (a) Punjab (b) Tamil Nadu
   (c) Rajasthan (d) Goa
4. Bihu is a festival celebrated in which state?
   (a) Assam (b) Kerala (c) Gujarat (d) Delhi
5. Which festival is known as the Festival of Lights?
   (a) Holi (b) Pongal (c) Diwali (d) Eid
6. What is the main language spoken in West Bengal?
   (a) Kannada (b) Bengali (c) Telugu (d) Marathi
7. Where shall you find this world famous monument?
   (a) Agra (b) Lucknow
   (c) Delhi (d) Hyderabad

8. Kathak is a classical dance form mainly from which region?
   (a) North India (b) South India
   (c) East India (d) West India
9. Which Union Territory is known for beaches and churches?
   (a) Ladakh (b) Delhi
   (c) Puducherry (d) Chandigarh
10. Onam is a famous harvest festival of which state?
    (a) Haryana (b) Kerala (c) Bihar (d) Sikkim

11. Which state is known as the "Land of Rising Sun" in India?
(a) Arunachal Pradesh
(b) Gujarat
(c) Tamil Nadu
(d) Rajasthan

12. Garba is a traditional dance of which state?
(a) Odisha
(b) Gujarat
(c) Assam
(d) Punjab

13. In which state are you most likely to find such a natural bridge?

(a) Bihar
(b) Meghalaya
(c) Gujarat
(d) Punjab

14. This is a famous festival of which state?

(a) Assam
(b) Nagaland
(c) Telangana
(d) Odisha

15. The given colonial era building is found in which state?

(a) Bihar
(b) West Bengal
(c) Odisha
(d) Manipur

16. Which state shall you visit to see this Minar?

(a) Maharashtra
(b) Telangana
(c) Andhra Pradesh
(d) Gujarat

17. Sri Vijaya Puram is the capital of which state/ UT?
(a) Lakshadweep
(b) Andaman & Nicobar
(c) Ladakh
(d) Mizoram

18. I am a Union Territory and capital of two states? Who am I?
(a) Puducherry
(b) New Delhi
(c) Chandigarh
(d) Ladakh

19. Where shall you find this monument?

(a) Mumbai
(b) Delhi
(c) Patna
(d) Hyderabad

20. Which state shall you visit to find this animal?

(a) Bihar
(b) Mizoram
(c) Assam
(d) Nagaland

2 Classical Dances of India

The 'Sangeet Natak Akademi' has recognised some dance forms as the classical dance forms of India. **Look at these pictures and name them correctly using the Help Box.**

1

2

3

4

5

6

7

Help Box

(a) Mohiniyattam
(b) Kuchipudi
(c) Manipuri
(d) Kathak
(e) Odissi
(f) Bharatanatyam
(g) Kathakali
(h) Sattriya

8

3 Ayurveda in Daily Life

Here are some tips from Ayurveda that you should follow every day to lead a healthy and happy life.

Wake up early in the morning, between 4:30 a.m. and 6:00 a.m. This is when our energy levels are the highest.

Drink a glass of water to flush out **toxins** from your body. If possible, drink water that has been boiled for **10 minutes** and brought down to room temperature.

Make sure to take out time to empty your **bladder and bowels**. Brush your teeth properly. Use a **tongue cleaner** as well.

Take a shower with clean **water**. Use a **soap**, shower gel or shampoo according to your dosha.

After wearing fresh and clean clothes, say a prayer for two minutes and thank God for everything.

Stimulate your six senses with every meal by always introducing all six tastes (sweet, sour, salty, spicy, bitter and astringent). Each of these tasks has different effects on the body and mind.

Always try to eat freshly cooked food. Not only it is healthier, but also tastes better.

Always drink warm water between meals. It makes our digestive tract stronger.

Maintain a daily routine. Follow the Ayurvedic approach to set your routine.

Note: *Dosha* in Ayurveda is that 'which can cause problem' to your mind and body.

4 Floor Decorations

Rangoli is an art form that is used to decorate the floor of houses. It is a symbol of religion and culture in India. Rangoli is made using ground rice, coloured sand or even flower petals.

Read the clues and name the floor decoration using the Help Box.

1

It includes colourful images of gods and goddesses drawn on the floor of the *kalam*.

2

This in Karnataka, uses one to nine dots to make a design.

3

It is an art form from Chhattisgarh.

4

In West Bengal this is designed using a thin paste of rice powder in water.

5

This is a floor art form in Rajasthan.

6

This in Bihar, was initially designed to thank God for a good harvest.

This in Odisha, is drawn to make a connection between God and the material world.

7

8

This is a floor art form practised in Maharashtra.

This one is from Tamil Nadu.

9
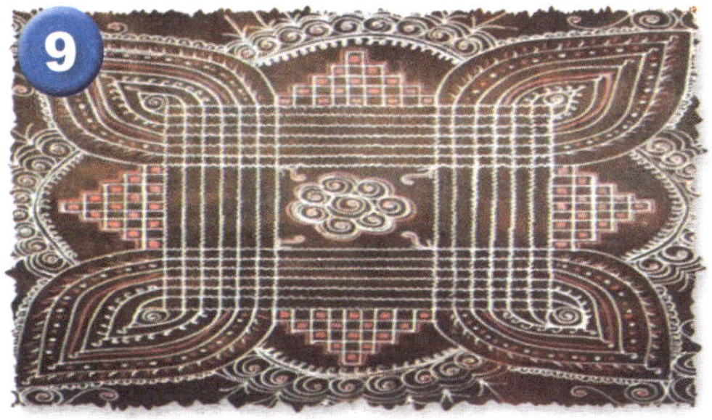

10

It is drawn using *muggu pindi*.

This one is from Himachal Pradesh.

11

12

It is made during the Onam festival.

Help Box

(a) Kalamezhuthu	(e) Rangoli	(i) Chaowkpurana
(b) Alpana	(f) Mandana	(j) Aripan
(c) Murja	(g) Sanskar Bharti	(k) Kolam
(d) Muggulu	(h) Aipan	(l) Pookolam

1	2	3	4	5	6	7	8	9	10	11	12

5 National Symbols of India

Each country has special symbols that represent its culture, heritage, and values. Let's learn about the national symbols of our country — India!

1. **National Flag – Tiranga**
   - It has **three horizontal stripes**:
     Saffron (top): Courage and strength
     White (middle): Peace and truth
     Green (bottom): Growth and prosperity
   - In the middle, there is a **blue Ashoka Chakra** (wheel) with **24 spokes**.

2. **National Anthem – Jana Gana Mana**
   - Written by **Rabindranath Tagore**.

3. **National Song – Vande Mataram**
   - Written by **Bankim Chandra Chatterjee**.

4. **National Emblem – The Lion Capital of Ashoka**
   - Below it is the motto: **"Satyameva Jayate"** — which means Truth Alone Triumphs.

5. **National Animal – Tiger**
   - The **Royal Bengal Tiger** is our national animal.

6. **National Bird – Peacock**

7. **National Flower – Lotus**
   - It stands for purity and beauty.

8. **National Tree – Banyan Tree**

9. **National Currency – Indian Rupee (₹)**

10. **National Fruit – Mango**

Quiz Time

Tick the correct answer.

1. Which national symbol of India can "scream" loud enough to scare off a predator?
   (a) National Fruit (b) National Animal (c) National Bird (d) National Flower
2. Our national heritage animal was picked because it behaves like a chill elder. What is it?
   (a) Asiatic Lion (b) Indian Elephant (c) Dolphin (d) Nilgai
3. Which national symbol is not from the natural world?
   (a) Peacock (b) Tiger
   (c) Lotus (d) National Emblem
4. The national flag's Ashoka Chakra was taken from a wheel that originally symbolised
   (a) Time (b) Law and Justice (c) War (d) Royal power
5. Which national symbol literally appears on money, passports, and government buildings—but started from an ancient pillar?
   (a) National Song (b) National Emblem (c) National Animal (d) National Flower
6. The national aquatic animal of India uses sound clicks like a tiny underwater radar. Who is it?
   (a) Olive Ridley Turtle (b) Ganges River Dolphin (c) Pufferfish (d) Flying Fish
7. Which national symbol is linked to purity because it grows even in muddy water?
   (a) Lotus (b) Jasmine (c) Marigold (d) Rose
8. Imagine you see a bird spreading its feathers in a full rainbow fan. What national symbol is that?
   (a) Kingfisher (b) Peacock (c) Duck (d) Egret
9. You spot a giant tree with hanging roots, where birds are chilling, kids are playing. Which national symbol is it?
   (a) Neem (b) Peepal (c) Banyan (d) Teak

6 Food from South India

When we think about South Indian cuisine, images of *idli, sambhar, vada* and *dosa* come flashing in our minds. But there are more varieties of cuisines in South India, made rich with flavours using spices and local ingredients.

Kerala

Idiyappam is 'string hoppers' made from rice flour. It is a traditional steamed rice noodle.

Injipuli is a dark brown sweet-sour and spicy Kerala curry made with ginger, tamarind, green chillies and jaggery.

Telangana

Puntikura chana dal also called *gongura pappu,* is made by boiling red sorrel leaves and *toor* or *chana dal* in a pressure cooker. Later, spices, curry leaves, salt and tempering are added to it.

Sarva pindi is a salty pancake made of rice flour, spices and peanuts. It is also called *tappala cheka.*

Karnataka

AKKI ROTTI

Akki rotti is 'rice bread'. a typical breakfast item in Karnataka. It is made of rice flour mixed with salt and water, kneaded into a dough and patted flat, directly cooked on the *tava*.

RAGI MUDDE

Ragi mudde is made of *ragi* (finger millet) flour and water. The mixture is boiled and beaten into a smooth dough. It is allowed to cool and made into balls. It is eaten with *rasam* or *sambar*.

Tamil Nadu

AVIAL

Avial is a thick mixture of vegetables and coconut, seasoned with coconut oil and curry leaves.

MURUKKU

Murukku is a fried savoury and crunchy snack. In Tamil, *Murukku* means 'twisted'. It is made of rice flour, *urad dal flour* and salt.

Andhra Pradesh

CHEPALA PULUSU

Chepala pulusu is a tangy Andhra-style fish curry cooked in tamarind paste.

PESARAATTU

Pesaraattu is a dish similar to *dosa*. It is made with the batter of green gram dal.

AI Powered QUIZZES

SECTION QUIZ

Scan the QR code to take the quiz on the section Amazing India'

CODE-DcsG

7 Continents and Oceans

There are seven continents in the world.

S. No.	Continents	Interesting Facts
1.	Asia	• Home to the world's highest peak, **Mount Everest (8,848 m)**. • The **Yangtze River** is Asia's longest river (6,300 km).
2.	Africa	• The **Nile** is the **world's longest river** (about 6,650 km). • Africa has the **largest desert**, the **Sahara**, almost the size of the USA.
3.	North America	• The **Mississippi-Missouri river system** is one of the world's longest. • **Greenland**, the world's largest island, belongs to North America.
4.	South America	• The **Amazon Rainforest** produces about **20% of the world's oxygen**. • The **Andes** is the **longest continental mountain range** (about 7,000 km).
5.	Antarctica	• Coldest and driest continent on Earth. • Holds about 70% of the world's freshwater (frozen as ice).
6.	Europe	• The Danube flows through 10 countries, more than any other river.
7.	Australia (Oceania)	• Australia is the smallest continent, but the largest island. • Home to unique animals like kangaroos, koalas, etc.

Oceans

There are five oceans in the world.

S. No.	Oceans	Interesting Facts
1.	Pacific Ocean	• Contains the **Mariana Trench**, the deepest part of the Earth. • The **"Ring of Fire"** surrounds it — an area of frequent earthquakes and volcanoes.
2.	Atlantic Ocean	• Site of the **Titanic's** sinking in 1912. • Known for the **Bermuda Triangle**, a region of mysterious disappearances.
3.	Indian Ocean	• Warmest of all oceans.
4.	Southern (Antarctic) Ocean	• Officially recognised as the **fifth ocean** in 2000. • Vital for regulating the Earth's **climate and carbon balance**.
5.	Arctic Ocean	• Covered by **sea ice** most of the year. • Rich in **marine life** and potential energy resources.

Quiz Time

Tick the correct answer.

1. Which continent is shaped almost like a triangle and is home to the Sahara Desert?
   (a) Asia (b) Africa (c) South America (d) Europe
2. The Pacific Ocean is so big that it's larger than all the continents combined. Which of these islands is NOT in the Pacific Ocean?
   (a) Fiji (b) Hawaii (c) Madagascar (d) Philippines
3. Which continent has no desert at all?
   (a) Africa (b) Antarctica (c) Europe (d) Australia
4. Which ocean is the saltiest?
   (a) Atlantic (b) Indian (c) Arctic (d) Pacific
5. Which continent is nicknamed the "Dark Continent"?
   (a) Africa (b) Asia (c) South America (d) Europe
6. The longest mountain range in the world is under which ocean?
   (a) Atlantic (b) Indian (c) Pacific (d) Arctic
7. Which continent is the only one to be entirely in the Southern Hemisphere?
   (a) Africa (b) Australia (c) South America (d) Asia
8. If you wanted to travel across the world's largest ocean, which ocean would you cross?
   (a) Indian (b) Atlantic (c) Pacific (d) Arctic
9. Which continent has the most countries?
   (a) Africa (b) Europe (c) Asia (d) South America

8 Countries and Their Capitals

Here is the list of some famous countries, their capitals with pictures of famous monuments and unique facts associated with each of them. Write the correct number from Help Box to match each one.

1 India – New Delhi

2 Australia – Canberra

3 United States of America – Washington, D.C.

4 United Kingdom – London

5 France – Paris

6 China – Beijing

7 Japan – Tokyo

8 Italy – Rome

9 Indonesia – Jakarta

10 Egypt – Cairo

11 Brazil – Brasília

12 Russia – Moscow

13 Canada – Ottawa

14 Thailand – Bangkok

15 Saudi Arabia – Riyadh

Help Box

(a) The Forbidden City

(b) Eiffel Tower

(c) Elizabeth Tower

(d) Qutub Minar

(e) White House

(f) Between Sydney and Melbourne

(g) Ultra-efficient and punctual transportation system

(h) 130 active volcanoes in the nation

(i) Colosseum

(j) Kremlin

(k) Great Pyramid of Giza

(l) Shaped like an airplane

(m) Located in a desert

(n) Longest city name

(o) Rideau canal

9 Nicknames

Many places and countries have nicknames because of certain unique qualities they possess. Match the nicknames with the places correctly.

Nickname	Place
1 City of Golden Gate	a Broadway
2 Emerald Isle	b Cuba
3 The Isle of Spring	c Palestine
4 Land of the Golden Pagoda	d Ireland
5 The Land Down Under	e Switzerland
6 The Saw Mill of Europe	f San Francisco
7 Great White Way	g Jamaica
8 Holy Land	h Myanmar
9 Sugar Bowl of the World	i Australia
10 Playground of Europe	j Sweden

Shwedagon Pagoda, Yangon, Myanmar

San Francisco

Sweden

Sydney Harbour, Australia

10 World Quiz

Give one-word answers for the following using the Help Box.

1. What is the Japanese art of flower arrangement called?
2. Name the national flower of Holland.
3. Where is Hagia Sophia?
4. Which Asian city's name literally means 'fragrant harbours'?
5. What is the parliament of Russia called?
6. Name the building constructed in 1930 that still stands in New York. It was the tallest building in the world when it was built.
7. Which canal links the Atlantic Ocean with the Pacific Ocean?
8. What are the native people of New Zealand called?
9. What are more than 20,000 islands scattered over the Pacific Ocean collectively called?
10. Where do Muslims go to perform Hajj?
11. In which country are the New Year celebrations marked by the Lantern Festival?
12. Name the Southeast Asian country where the traditional dance called *legong* is performed.

Maori

Kaaba

Help Box

(a) Indonesia
(b) Mecca
(c) Maori
(d) Chrysler Building
(e) Hong Kong
(f) Tulip
(g) Ikebana
(h) Istanbul
(i) Federal Assembly
(j) Panama Canal
(k) Oceania
(l) China

1	2	3	4	5	6	7	8	9	10	11	12

11 Places of Tourist Interest

There are many great buildings and monuments all over the world. They mark some important events or are related to some famous personalities.

Match the landmarks with the countries in which they are located.

Buckingham Palace

1 ______

Temple of Apollo

2 ______

Colosseum

4 ______

Machu Picchu

3 ______

Great Sphinx

5 ______

Help Box

(a) Greece (d) Egypt
(b) USA (e) UK
(c) Italy (f) Peru

Mount Rushmore

6 ______

AI Powered QUIZZES

SECTION QUIZ

Scan the QR code to take the quiz on the section 'Our Wonderful World'

CODE-5PCL

12 Natural Resources

Natural resources are the things we get from nature. They help us live and make our planet beautiful and healthy.

Three important natural resources are Land, **Air, and Water**. Read the features and write 'L' for land, 'A' for air and 'W' for water.

Land

Air

Water

1. It is the ground we walk, play, and build houses on.
2. It is needed for drinking, cooking, bathing, and cleaning.
3. We should not waste it while bathing or washing.
4. We must keep our rivers and ponds clean.
5. It is all around us, even though we can't see it.
6. Farmers grow fruits, vegetables, and crops.
7. Cutting too many trees and throwing garbage can spoil it.
8. We need it to breathe and live.
9. Plants, animals, and humans – all need it.
10. We get it from rain, rivers, lakes, and wells.
11. Smoke from cars and factories makes it dirty.
12. We should avoid burning waste to keep it clean.

13 Save Paper

Millions of trees are cut down every year to make paper. To save them, we can recycle the waste paper.

Four children are shown below. They do different activities. Points have been given to their activities. Add or deduct the points in their respective scores to find out which child is the most aware about environment.

To save paper, Abhinav writes on both sides of a sheet.

Add 6 Points

Rahul knows that recycling prevents wastage and reduces energy usage.

Add 6 Points

Rosy knows that processing old materials into new products is called recycling.

Add 6 Points

Chhavi always uses old newspapers and calendar sheets to cover her books.

Add 6 Points

Rahul reuses gift-wrapping papers.

Add 4 Points

Chhavi does not reuse paper bags and cartons.

Deduct 3 Points

Abhinav went to a recycling unit with his father to learn how to recycle paper.

Add 6 Points

Rosy loves to talk about environmental issues with her teachers and friends.

Add 6 Points

Abhinav loves drawing and painting. Most of the time, he draws and paints at the back of waste papers.

Add 6 Points

Rahul sells his old notebooks and newspapers to a scrap dealer to be sold to a recycling unit.

Add 4 Points

Rosy always tries to learn how she can save paper, as well as our beautiful Earth.

Add 6 Points

Chhavi's father works on a computer. She insists that he takes printouts only on single side of a paper.

Deduct 3 Points

DID YOU KNOW?

About 400 newspapers can be made from the wood pulp of one tree.

Abhinav

TOTAL

Rahul

TOTAL

Rosy

TOTAL

Chhavi

TOTAL

14 Waste! Waste!

Wastes are of two types—biodegradable and non-biodegradable. Biodegradable wastes can easily rot, and decompose while non-biodegradable wastes do not.

Identify the household wastes. Write 'B' for biodegradable and 'NB' for non-biodegradable wastes in the space given below.

1

2

3

4

5

6

7

8

9

10

11

12

AI Powered QUIZZES

SECTION QUIZ

Scan the QR code to take the quiz on the section 'Living With Nature'

CODE-pFqu

15 Flightless Birds

The birds that cannot fly are called flightless birds.

Identify the flightless birds using the Help Box.

1

2

3

4

5

DID YOU KNOW?

A bird named Clark's Nutcracker hides its food in thousands of places. It can recall exactly where it buried each food item up to nine months.

7

6

8

9

Help Box

(a) Weka	(d) Kiwi	(g) Penguin
(b) Kakapo	(e) Ostrich	(h) Emu
(c) Tahake	(f) Steamer Duck	(i) Cassowary

16 Animals Facts

Read the given facts on animals and fill in the boxes using the Help Box.

1

Fastest Land Animal

Fact: It can run up to 110 kilometres per hour — that's faster than a car in the city! It can reach that speed in just a few seconds — like a rocket on legs!

Fastest Sea Animal

Fact: It can swim at 110 kilometres per hour! It has a long, pointed nose that helps it move super fast through water.

2

3

Fastest Bird

Fact: When it dives to catch its prey, it can go faster than 300 kilometres per hour.

That makes it the fastest animal in the whole world!

4

Biggest Land Animal

Fact: The elephant can weigh up to 6,000 kilograms (that's like 100 kids together). It has big ears that help it stay cool in the hot sun.

5

Biggest Animal in the World

Fact: It is even bigger than any dinosaur! It can grow up to 30 metres long — that's as long as three school buses.

6

Smallest Mammal

Fact: This bat weighs less than a coin.

It lives in caves in Thailand and Myanmar.

7

Smallest Bird

Fact: It is only 5 centimetres long — smaller than your thumb.

Its wings beat about 80 times every second!

Help Box

(a) Bee Humming bird
(b) Blue whale
(c) Bumblebee Bat
(d) African elephant
(e) Sailfish
(f) Peregrine Falcon
(g) Cheetah

17 Misleading Names

Many animals and birds have strange names. Some names are actually 'misleading'.

Fill in the blank boxes.

1 ______________________

This **pig** is actually a **rodent**. The wild guinea is native to Brazil and not New Guinea. It is not a **pig**, but it does squeal like a **pig**.

2 ______________________

Despite having the word 'panda' in its name, it is not a panda. Sometimes, it is called **red cat panda**, but it is not a cat either. It is closely related to the raccoons.

3 ______________________

It seems to be a chicken species from some hilly area. But it is actually a frog! Officially named the giant **ditch frog** this frog is found in Dominica and Montserrat.

4 ____________

These bats belong to a group that scientists call **megabats**. They are also often known as **fruit** bats as they love to feed on **fruits**, flowers and nectar. They are called so because their heads look similar to those of foxes.

5 ____________

They are not really fish, as a fish's anatomy is centred around its backbone. It is actually a **dome-shaped invertebrate**.

Help Box

(a) Flying Fox
(b) Jelly Fish
(c) Tarantula Hawk
(d) Mountain Chicken
(e) Red Panda
(f) Guinea Pig

6 ____________

It is neither a tarantula, nor a hawk. It is a **spider wasp** that preys on tarantulas.

18 Rare Flowers

Let us learn about some rare flowers of the world. Name these on the basis of the given clues.

It is the rarest rose in the world. It took 15 years for rose breeder David Austin to cultivate this flower in England.

The orchid plant has no leaves and does not manufacture its own food. It gives a soap-like odour while blooming.

WOW!

The heads of **sunflowers** move throughout the day to follow the route of the Sun from east to west.

This lily is a rare flower. It is toxic to humans and can also cause skin irritation. It can grow up to 12 feet.

Its history can be traced to Japan, where they are known as *gekka bijin* or 'beauty under the moon'. These grow mainly in the wild among decaying matter around trees. These flowers can measure up to 30 cm in length and 17 cm in width.

These flowers are very rare. They bloom once in a few decades. Flocks of people gather at the botanical gardens to see these flowers. It is strange that people are willing to spend time and energy to smell something like rotten meat.

This Cosmos blooms in the forests of Mexico. This flower smells like chocolate.

Help Box

(a) Corpse Flower
(b) Chocolate Cosmos
(c) Kadupul Flower
(d) Fire Lily
(e) Ghost Orchid
(f) Juliet Rose

19 Strange Truths About Plants

Here are some strange truths about plants.

Onions contain a mild antibiotic that soothes burns, fights infections and relieves itching in the feet.

Avocado has the highest number of calories in fruits. These are approximately, 167 calories per hundred grams.

About 84% of a raw apple and 96% of a raw **cucumber** is water.

The family of **rose** plants also give us apples, pears, plums, cherries, almonds, peaches and apricots.

Peanuts are beans.

A **pineapple** is a berry.

AI Powered QUIZZES

SECTION QUIZ

Scan the QR code to take the quiz on the section 'Green and Wild'

CODE-xSwT

20 Symbols and Signs

Where would you find the following symbols or signs?

Match the pictures with the correct words.

Help Box

(a) National Mourning
(b) Use Me
(c) Keep Silence
(d) Danger
(e) You May Go
(f) Victory
(g) Peace or Surrender
(h) Do Not Feed Animals
(i) Housefull
(j) Medical Attention

1 **Library**

2 **Dustbin**

3 **Electric Wires**

4 **Zoo**

5 **Theatre**

6 **V-sign**

7 **White Flag**

8 **Green Flag**

9 **Half-mast Flag**

10 **Red Cross**

21 Places Located in Our Surroundings

These are certain important places located in our surroundings such as School, Hospital, Post Office, Police Station, Fire Station and Park. Read the given clues related to these and write S for School, H for Hospital, PO for Post Office, PS for Police Station, FS Fire station and P for Park.

1. School

2. Hospital

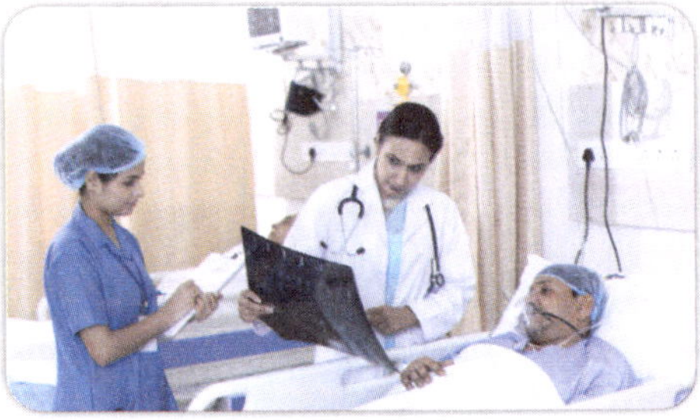

3. Post Office

4. Police Station

5. Fire Station

6. Park

1. This is where firefighters stay ready to put out fires and help in emergencies. ☐
2. This is a place where policemen and policewomen work to keep us safe. ☐
3. This is a place where we send and receive letters, parcels, and money orders. ☐
4. It is a place where doctors and nurses take care of sick or injured people. ☐
5. It is a place where children go to learn reading, writing, math, and science. ☐
6. They give us a place to exercise, relax, and enjoy nature. ☐

AI Powered QUIZZES

SECTION QUIZ

Scan the QR code to take the quiz on the section 'Exploring Our Surroundings'

CODE-qviK

22 Components of Balanced Diet

A **balanced diet** means **eating the right types and amounts of food** so that our body can grow, stay strong, and healthy. It includes **different kinds of food** that give us energy, help us grow, and protect us from diseases.

Fill in the blanks using the Help Box.

1. Carbohydrates – Energy-Giving Foods

Examples: Rice, bread, chapati, potatoes, sugar, cereals

Work: Carbohydrates give us __________ to run, play, and study.

2. Proteins – Body-Building Foods

Examples: Milk, eggs, fish, pulses (dal), beans, meat, nuts

Work: Proteins help us **grow, build muscles,** and __________ our body when we get hurt.

3. Fats – Energy-Storing Foods

Examples: Butter, ghee, oil, cheese, nuts, avocado

Work: Fats give us extra energy and help keep us ___________.

4. Vitamins – Protective Foods

Examples: Fruits and ________________ like oranges, carrots, spinach, tomato

Work: Vitamins keep our **eyes, skin, and body healthy** and protect us from ______________.

5. Minerals – Protective Foods

Examples: Milk (calcium), salt (iodine), fruits, vegetables

Work: Minerals help make **bones** _________, **teeth healthy**, and keep the body working properly.

6. Water – Protective Foods

Examples: Plain water, fruits like watermelon and cucumber

Work: Water helps hydrate muscles, **digest food, carry nutrients,** and _________ **waste** from our body.

Help Box

(a) Vegetables	(b) Diseases	(c) Strong	(d) Remove
(e) Energy	(f) Repair	(g) Warm	

23 Should I? Shouldn't I?

All of us must follow healthy habits. Read these sentences and fill in the blanks using 'should' or 'shouldn't.

1

You ___________ eat healthy food.

2

You ___________ drink enough water.

3

You _______ watch television for long hours.

4

You ___________ play a sport.

5

You ___________ brush your teeth at least twice a day.

6

You ___________ eat junk food.

7

You ___________ wash your hands regularly.

AI Powered QUIZZES

SECTION QUIZ

Scan the QR code to take the quiz on the section 'Health and Happiness'

CODE-w1FA

Check Point Test-1

(Based on pages 4 to 37)

A. Give your answer in one word.

1. Garba is the traditional dance of which state? ____________
2. What is the floor decoration in Kerala called? ____________
3. Name the national bird of India. ____________
4. Where is *sarva pindi* cooked? ____________
5. Where is the 'Ring of Fire' located. ____________

B. Write two examples of each.

1. Foods from South India ____________ ____________
2. Oceans around the world ____________ ____________
3. Continents ____________ ____________
4. Flightless birds ____________ ____________
5. Rare flowers ____________ ____________

C. Tick (✓) the correct choice.

1. Which kind of food is a pineapple?

   ◯ berry ◯ beans ◯ cereal

2. Where is the Colosseum located?

   ◯ Greece ◯ Italy ◯ Egypt

3. Name the country where Kiwi bird is found.

   ◯ Finland ◯ Sweden ◯ New Zealand

4. Ayurveda is called the Science of

   ◯ Life ◯ Healing ◯ Surgery

5. Name the fastest bird.

   ◯ Eagle ◯ Bat ◯ Peregrine falcon

D. **Identify the following.**

1. ____________ 2. ____________ 3. ____________

4. ____________ 5. ____________ 6. ____________

E. **Write 'T' for True and 'F' for False.**

1. Capital of Thailand is Bangkok.
2. Tahake is a flightless bird.
3. The Mountain Chicken is a chicken species from a hilly area.
4. Machu Pichu is in Greece.
5. Juliet rose is the rarest rose in the world.

F. **Fill in the blanks.**

1. ____________ is a thick mixture of vegetables and coconut dish from Tamil Nadu.
2. The Titanic sank in ____________ ocean.
3. Our National Tree is ____________ .
4. The Great Sphinx is in ____________.
5. ____________ is a dome-shaped invertebrate.

24 I.Q. Challenge 1

Find the figure which will complete the problem figure.

1. Problem figure:

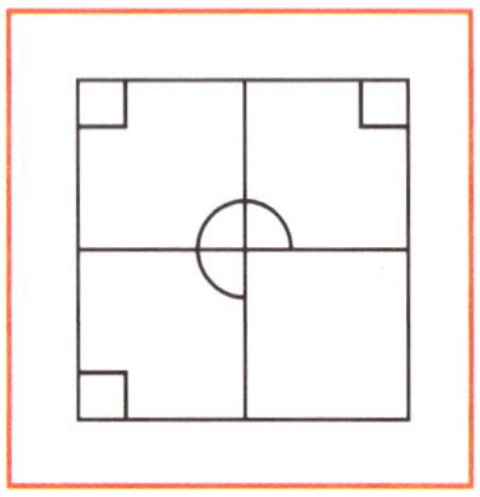

(a)

(b)

(c)

(d)

2. Problem figure:

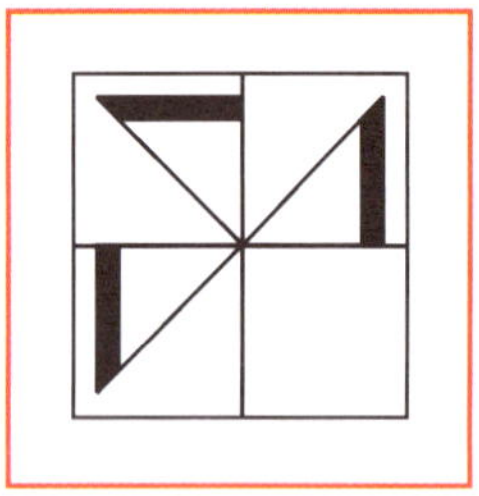

(a)

(b)

(c)

(d)

Find the figure which resembles the given problem figure.

3. Problem figure:

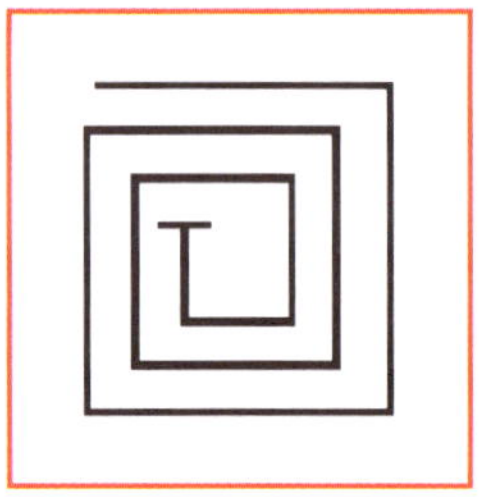

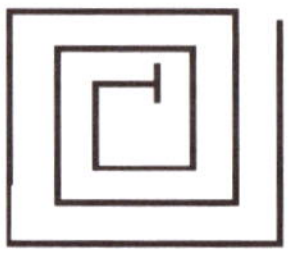

(a)

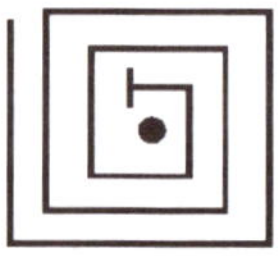

(b)

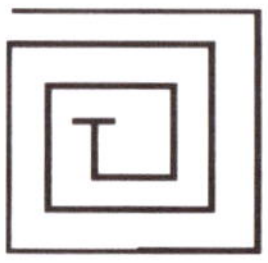

(c)

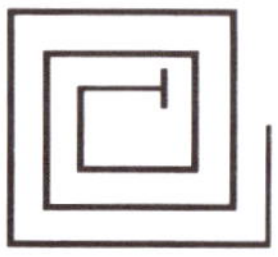

(d)

4. Problem figure:

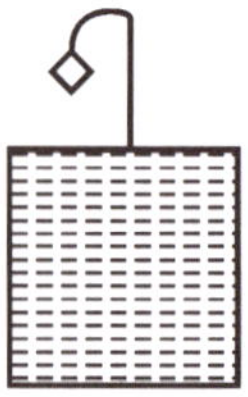

(a)

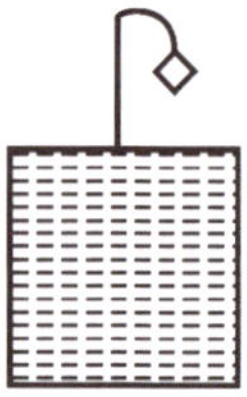

(b)

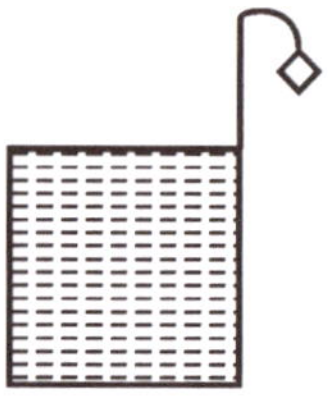

(c)

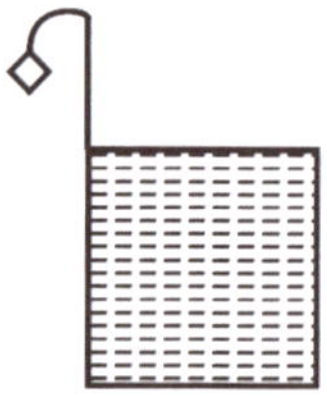

(d)

25 I.Q. Challenge 2

Find the odd one out.

1.

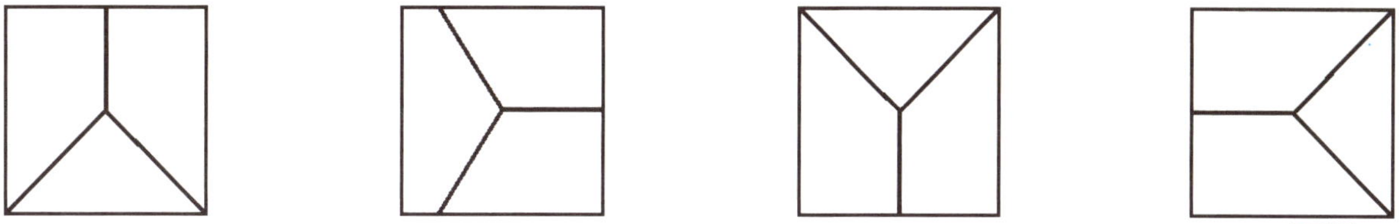

(a) (b) (c) (d)

2.

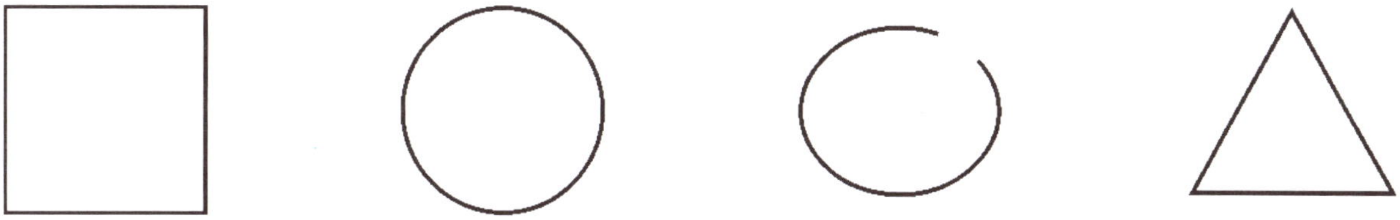

(a) (b) (c) (d)

Find the figure which completes the problem figure.

3. Problem figure:

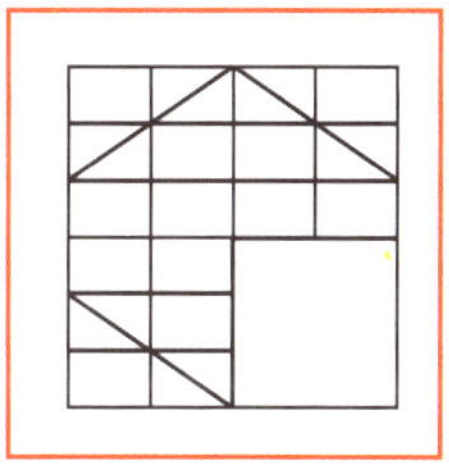

(a) (b) (c) (d)

4. Problem figure:

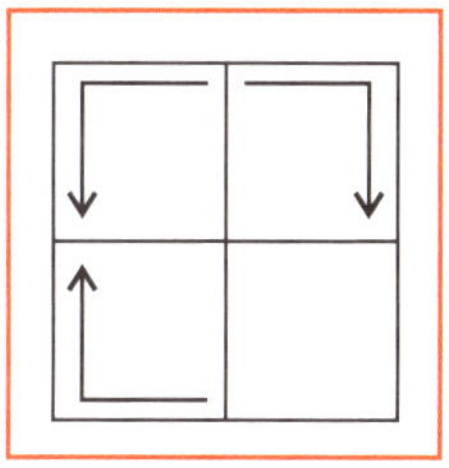

(a) (b) (c) (d)

Find the figure which resembles the given problem figure :

5. Problem figure:

(a) (b) (c) (d)

26 Quiz 1

Tick the correct answer.

1. In which continent is the world's longest river, the Nile, located?

   (a) Africa (b) Australia (c) Asia

2. Which continent lies to the east of Europe?

   (a) Australia (b) Africa (c) Asia

3. Which among the following is the highest waterfall in the world?

   (a) Niagara Falls (b) Angel Falls (c) Yosemite Falls

4. Which is the world's largest country by area?

   (a) USA (b) Russia (c) UK

5. In which continent is the world's largest desert, the Sahara, located?

   (a) Africa (b) Europe (c) Asia

6. Which continent contains about 80 per cent of freshwater present on the Earth?

   (a) Asia (b) Antarctica (c) Australia

7. What are icebergs made up of?

   (a) freshwater (b) seawater (c) groundwater

8. In what form is water most abundant on Earth?

   (a) snow (b) seawater (c) freshwater

9. Which among the following is the island continent in the world?

   (a) Greenland (b) Malaysia (c) Australia

10. Which is the world's largest glacier?

    (a) Lambert glacier (b) Biafo glacier (c) Yalung glacier

27 Being Sensitive

Being sensitive towards people means being careful and thoughtful of our words and actions, as they can impact them.

Be polite to everyone.

Don't tease anyone for being tall, fat, short or thin.

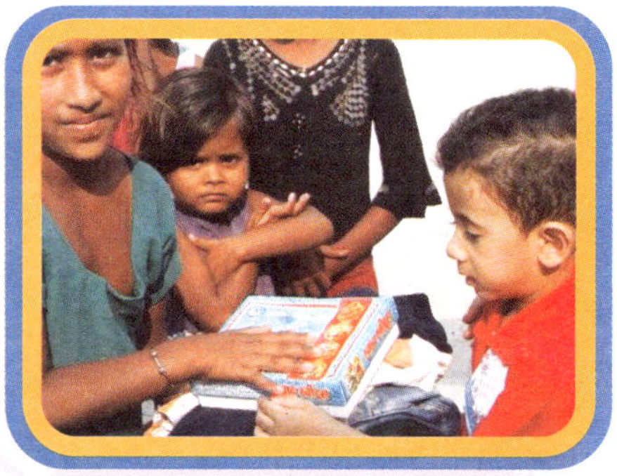

Never treat a poor person badly. Be kind and helpful.

Include new students as your friends in class.

Don't laugh if someone falls down. Help him/ her get up.

Don't treat someone rudely just because of complexion. God made all of us equal.

The best way to be sensitive is to put yourself in another person's place and think about how she/he feels about your behaviour or words.

28 Be a Smart Child

What would you do in the following situations?

Tick (✓) the correct option in each situation to be a smart child.

1

If you meet someone in the park

you would greet him/her.

you would smile and go away from there.

2

If you need to interrupt someone

you would say — Excuse Me.

you would interrupt him/her without saying anything.

3

If you are going to a crowded place with your parents

you would ask your parents not to hold your hands.

you would stay close to your parents.

4

If your teacher is teaching in the classroom

- you would listen to him/her carefully.
- you would keep chatting with your friends.

5

If someone gives you a gift

- you would ask about the price.
- you would say—Thank You.

6

If you need to cut something short

- you would bring a knife from the kitchen to cut it yourself.
- you would ask an adult to cut it short.

7

If you are about to sneeze

- you would sneeze without caring for anyone.
- you would use a handkerchief and say Excuse Me afterwards.

29 Empathy

Empathy is being able to know how someone else is feeling, even when you aren't in the same situation. Sometimes, in more simple words, we call empathy being able to "put yourself in someone's shoes" and see things from their view.

Empathy includes **Feeling, Thinking, Saying, and Doing.**

Make Emotion Flashcards like these. Add these details

Feelings Flashcards

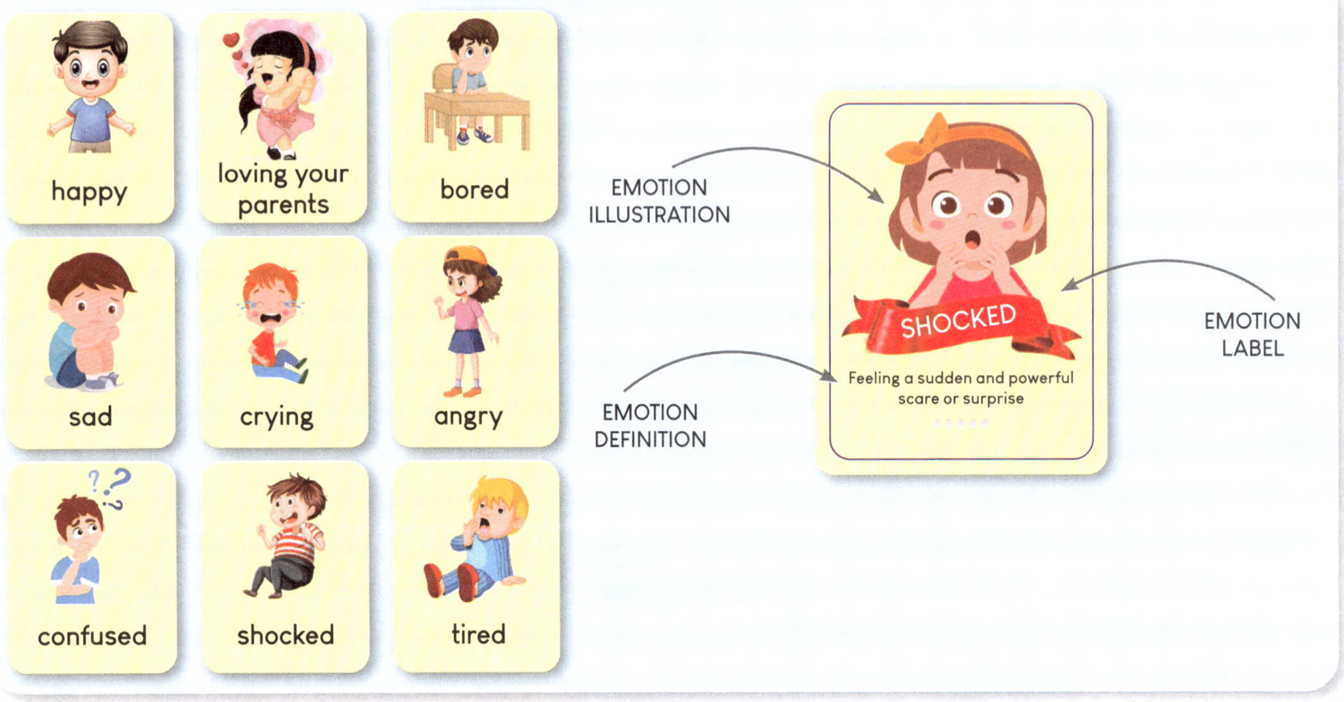

Now play these games.

Conversation Starters

Take turns picking a card from the deck. Read it aloud and share a situation when you experience that emotion with others.

Emotions Memory Game / Emotions Matching Game

Print two sets of flashcards. Place the cards facing down and take turns lifting any two cards. If the cards match, keep them and proceed to turn another two. If not, leave them facing down and let the next player take a turn. The player who gets more pairs at the end wins.

30 Yoga for Kids

Yoga originated in India. It is important to learn accurate postures of various yoga exercises to stay fit.

Remember that yoga should be practised under the guidance of an expert.

Tadasana (Palm Tree Posture)

- Promotes good posture
- Improves your flexibility
- Strengthens your legs and abdominal muscles

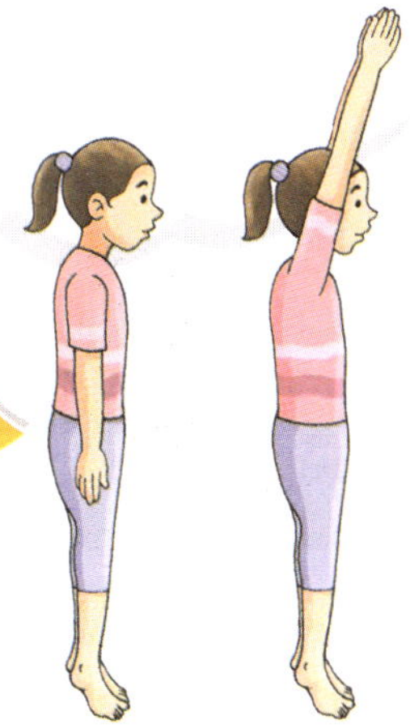

Hastottanasana (Upstretched Arms Posture)

- Stretches the muscles of the ribs
- Reduces pain in the neck, shoulders and arms
- Increases the height of children

Katichakrasana (Waist Twist Posture)

- Helps to stretch the waist
- Makes the waist more flexible and supple
- Helps to relieve constipation

Simhasana (Lion Posture)

- Releases excess energy
- Helps children connect with their inner strength
- Elevates your spirits

AI Powered QUIZZES

SECTION QUIZ

Scan the QR code to take the quiz on the section 'Skills for Life'

CODE-AYkT

31 Similies

Complete the following similies using the Help Box.

1. As ______________ as a dog
2. As busy as a ______________
3. As ______________ as a fox
4. As foolish as a ______________
5. As ______________ as a bat
6. As slow as a ______________
7. As ______________ as a horse
8. As gentle as a ______________
9. As ______________ as a lion
10. As sharp as a ______________
11. As ______________ as ABC
12. As sweet as ______________

Help Box

(a) bee	(d) lamb	(g) honey	(j) blind
(b) donkey	(e) brave	(h) knife	(k) sly
(c) snail	(f) easy	(i) strong	(l) faithful

32 Partnerships

There are well-known characters — animal or things, generally associated with each other.
Find out the second partner using the Help Box.

1. The Owl and ____________
2. Akbar and ____________
3. Lord Krishna and ____________
4. Androcles and ____________
5. Robin Hood and ____________
6. Snow White and ____________
7. Ali Baba and ____________
8. The Ramayana and ____________
9. The Pandavas and ____________
10. Laurel and ____________

DID YOU KNOW?

A story that uses animal characters to convey a message with moral value is called a *fable*.

Help Box

(a) the Lion	**(e)** the Pussy Cat	**(i)** the Seven Dwarfs
(b) Hardy	**(f)** Birbal	**(j)** the Forty Thieves
(c) Arjuna	**(g)** the Mahabharata	
(d) the Kauravas	**(h)** his Merry Men	

33 Pairs

Fill in the blanks with suitable pairing words, using the Help Box.

1. Body and ______________________
2. Pins and ______________________
3. Sword and ______________________
4. Head and ______________________
5. Part and ______________________
6. Tooth and ______________________
7. Bag and ______________________
8. Roots and ______________________
9. Heads and ______________________
10. Lock and ______________________
11. Heaven and ______________________
12. Thunder and ______________________

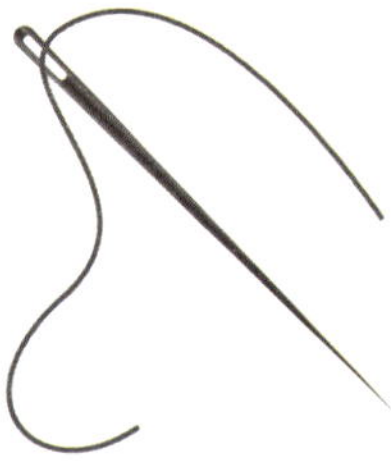

Help Box

(a) key	**(d)** needles	**(g)** shoulders	**(j)** lightning
(b) shield	**(e)** Earth	**(h)** tails	**(k)** baggage
(c) soul	**(f)** nail	**(i)** parcel	**(l)** branch

34 Words for Groups

Sometimes, a noun is used for a collection or a group of things. It is called a collective noun.

Complete each phrase with a suitable collective noun using the Help Box.

1. A ______________ of monkeys
2. A ______________ of fish
3. A ______________ of clothes
4. A ______________ of stones
5. A ______________ of pearls
6. A ______________ of eggs
7. A ______________ of names
8. A ______________ of bananas
9. A ______________ of flowers
10. A ______________ of stairs
11. A ______________ of crockery
12. A ______________ of puppies
13. A ______________ of cards
14. A ______________ of birds
15. A ______________ of sticks

DID YOU KNOW?

The Earth's seven billion people speak more than 7,000 languages.

FUNNY FACT

A baker's dozen has 13 eggs.

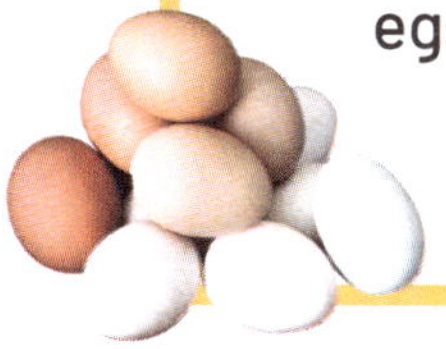

Help Box

(a) set	(e) shoal	(i) bunch	(m) string
(b) pack	(f) comb	(j) flight	(n) flock
(c) litter	(g) troop	(k) bundle	(o) heap
(d) list	(h) clutch	(l) wardrobe	

35 Colourful Phrases

Read the following phrases and fill in the correct colour names using the Help Box. Find out the meanings of the phrases.

1. Out of the ______________________.
2. Get the ______________________ light.
3. ______________________ bellied.
4. In a ______________________ study.
5. In a ______________________ mood.
6. Seeing ______________________.
7. In the ______________________ of good health.
8. Born to the ______________________.
9. Lay it on in ______________________.
10. ______________________ elephant.
11. ______________________ sheep.
12. The ______________________ Screen.
13. The ______________________ opportunity.

Help Box

(a) green	(f) Black	(k) blue
(b) brown	(g) lavender	(l) golden
(c) red	(h) pink	(m) silver
(d) purple	(i) grey	
(e) white	(j) yellow	

DID YOU KNOW?

The longest English word without a vowel is RHYTHM.

AI Powered QUIZZES

SECTION QUIZ

Scan the QR code to take the quiz on the section 'Tales and Texts'

CODE-sDBj

36 World of Musical Instruments

Music is a universally understood language. Musicians in different countries and cultures use different instruments to create their unique music.

How many can you name correctly?

1 ______

2 ______

3 ______

4 ______

5 ______

6 ______

7 ______

8 ____________________

9 ____________________

10 ____________________

11 ____________________

12 ____________________

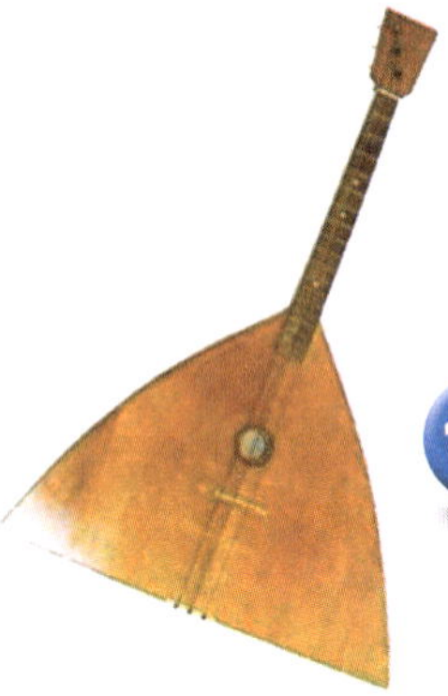

13 ____________________

14 ____________________

15 ____________________

Help Box

(a) Tar, Iran	(b) Balalaika, Russia	(c) Rubab, Afghanistan
(d) Bagpipe, Scotland	(e) Kalimba, South Africa	(f) Cas Cas Shaker, Africa
(g) Caxixi, Brazil	(h) Singing Bowl, Tibet	(i) Pan Flute, Bolivia
(j) Sitar, India	(k) Digeridoo, Australia	(l) Bodhran, Ireland
(m) Conga, Cuba	(n) Shamisen, Japan	(o) Wind Gong, Philippines

37 Sports And Entertainment

1. India Women's National Cricket Team — First Women's World Cup Title 2025

- The **2025 ICC Women's Cricket World Cup** was the 13th edition of Women's Cricket World Cup The Indian women's team won their **first ever** 2025 ICC Women's Cricket World Cup by beating South Africa in the final by 52 runs.

2. India Wins the 2025 ICC Champions Trophy

- The **2025 ICC Champions Trophy** was the ninth edition of the ICC Champions Trophy. It was hosted by Pakistan Cricket Board in February and March 2025 and featured 15 matches held across three venues in Pakistan and one in the United Arab Emirates.

3. India Men's National Cricket Team — Winning the T20 World Cup 2024

- In 2024, India won the 2024 ICC Men's T20 World Cup and became the first Asian team to win the T20 World Cup twice.

4. 2025 Archery World Cup Stage 2

- At the Archery World Cup Stage 2 in Shanghai (2025), India won **7 medals:** 2 gold, 1 silver, 4 bronze.

5. First-ever medals at the 2025 World Games

- At the 2025 World Games (Chengdu), India achieved its best-ever performance: 3 medals (1 silver, 2 bronze).

6. Big wins at the 2025 Asian Youth Games

- India secured a record 48 medals (13 gold, 18 silver, 17 bronze) at the 2025 Asian Youth Games in Manama, Bahrain.

Quiz Time

Tick the correct answer.

1. Who was the player of the match in the finals of Women's World Cup 2025?
   (a) Deepti Sharma (b) Shafali Verma
   (c) Smriti Mandhana (d) Ayabanga Khaka
2. Which team was the runners-up in 2025 ICC Champions Trophy?
   (a) India (b) New Zealand
   (c) Australia (d) Pakistan
3. Which team was the runners-up in 2025 ICC Wormen's Cricket World Cup?
   (a) Australia (b) South Africa
   (c) Pakistan (d) New Zealand
4. Which is the first Asian team to win ICC Men's T20 World Cup twice?
   (a) India (b) Pakistan
   (c) Sri Lanka (d) Bangladesh

38 To Play a Game

Can you match the game with the place where it is played?

Every game is played at a certain place. Each place where a particular game is played is known by a particular name.

Help Box

(a) Golf
(b) Cricket
(c) Swimming
(d) Tennis
(e) Boxing
(f) Cycling
(g) Skating
(h) Hockey

1 **Velodrome**

2 **Ring**

3 **Pitch**

4 **Court**

5 **Course**

6 **Rink**

7 **Astroturf**

8 **Pool**

DID YOU KNOW?

- The State Sport of Alabama is figure skating.
- The O-chimp-ics, a multi-sport international event for monkeys, was held every four years from 1952 to 1960.
- Kite flying is a professional sport in Thailand.

AI Powered QUIZZES

SECTION QUIZ

Scan the QR code to take the quiz on the section 'Fun and Fitness'

CODE-ksPS

39 Famous Inventions

Here is a list of some famous inventions. Write the name of the inventor in the given box.

1 Telephone

Fact: He made the first telephone in **1876** so that people could talk to each other even when they were far away. Without him, we wouldn't have mobile phones today!

2 Aeroplane

Fact: They made the first flying machine in **1903**. Their first flight lasted only **12 seconds**, but it changed the world!

3 Electric Bulb

Fact: He made a light bulb that could stay on for hours in **1879**. He helped people work after sunset.

4 Computer

Fact: He is called the "**Father of the Computer.**"

He designed the first idea of a computer in **1822**, long before real computers were built!

5 Internet

Fact: He invented the World Wide Web (WWW) in 1989.

6 Motor Car

Fact: He made the first petrol-powered car in **1886**. His company later became **Mercedes-Benz**, a famous car brand.

7 Telescope

Fact: He made a telescope in **1609** and was the first to see **mountains on the Moon!** He showed that space is full of wonders.

8 Radio

Fact: He sent the first radio signal across the Atlantic ocean in **1901**.

9 Vaccination

Fact: In **1796**, he made the first vaccine to eradicate smallpox, a deadly disease.

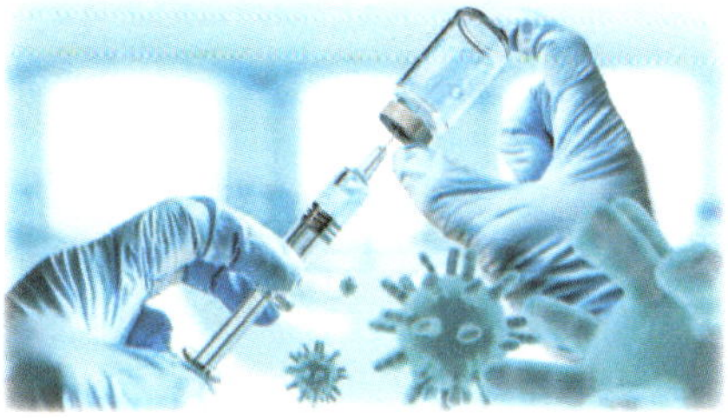

Help Box

(a) Edward Jenner	(b) Guglielmo Marconi	(c) Galileo Galilei	**(d)** Karl Benz
(e) Charles Babbage	**(f)** Thomas Alva Edison	(g) Wright Brothers	**(h)** Graham Bell
(i) Tim Berners-Lee			

40 The Sun's Family

Identify the members of the Sun's family.

1. This planet is named after the speedy messenger of the Gods. It is closest to the Sun.

M _ R C _ _ Y

2. It is similar to Earth in size. It is also known as the Morning and Evening Star.

_ E _ U _

3. We live on this planet. Water is found on it.

_ A _ T _

4. This planet is also known as the Red Planet.

_ A _ S

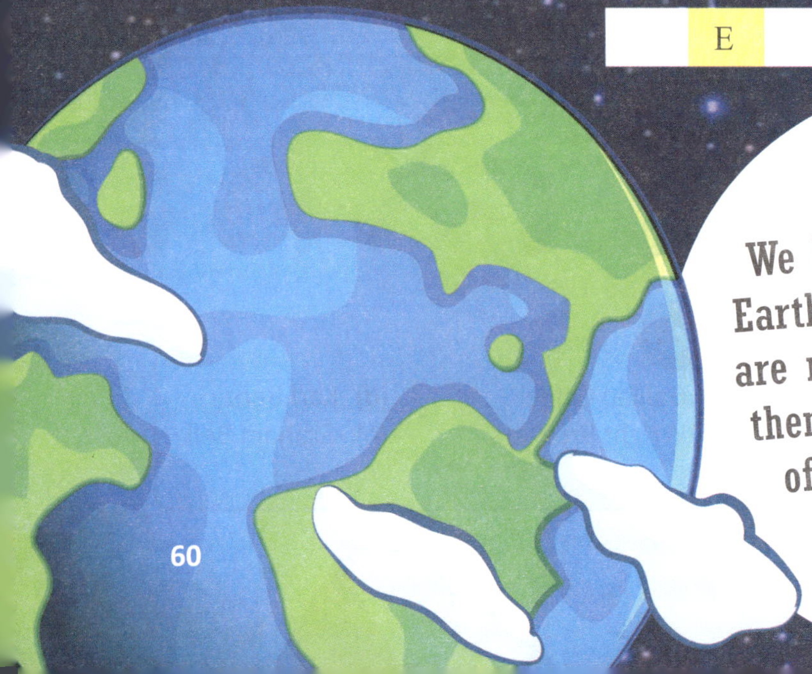

PLANET

We live on Earth. Our Earth is a planet. There are many planets. All of them are the members of the sun's family.

	R		N		S

6 It is bluish-green in colour.

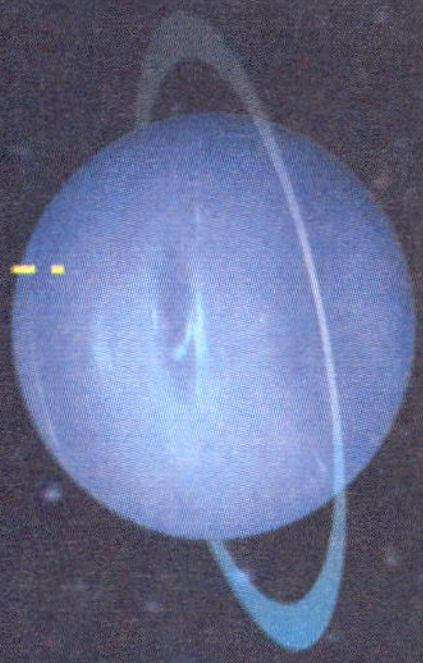

	U		I	T		R

5 It is the largest of all planets. It is big enough to contain more than one thousand Earths.

7 It is blue in colour. It is farthest from the sun.

N		P	T			E

8 It is the second largest planet. It is surrounded with rings.

S		T		R	

WOW!

The sun is 14,95,97,893 km from Earth and has a diameter of 13,91,940 km.

FUNNY FACT

Thomas Stafford, John Young and Gene Cernan were the crew members of NASA's Apollo 10 mission between 18-26 May 1969. They were the first men to shave in space.

Science Around Us

41 On the Screen

As soon as you start your computer, you see a number of icons or applications on the screen.

Identify the icons or programs shown here using the Help Box.

1 ____________

2 ____________

3 ____________

4 ____________

5 ____________

6 ____________

7 ____________

8 ____________

9 ____________

DID YOU KNOW?

In general, people tend to read as much as 10% slower on a screen than on paper.

Help Box

(a) MS Excel	(d) MS Word	(g) My Documents
(b) Notepad	(e) Paint	(h) Recycle Bin
(c) Microsoft Edge	(f) The PC	(i) PowerPoint

AI Powered QUIZZES

SECTION QUIZ

Scan the QR code to take the quiz on the section 'Science Around Us'

CODE-RLP4

42 Amazing Facts

Pandas have a sixth toe that they use for grasping bamboos.

Fish can cough.

Your nose gets a little warm when you lie.

Platypus is the only animal that has no stomach.

Horses and cows can sleep standing up.

Crabs taste food with their feet.

Octopuses have blue blood and nine brains.

Some **cat** breeds (called '**puppy cats**') are bred specifically to exhibit dog-like behaviour.

If you drive to the sun at 55mph, it would take you about 193 years

Magpies are considered one of the most intelligent animals in the world and the only non-mammal species that is able to recognise themselves in a mirror test.

There's a flower that smells like chocolate! Native to Mexico, this dark red flower is not edible. It is called *cosmos atrosanguineus* or '**chocolate cosmos**.'

AI Powered QUIZZES

SECTION QUIZ

Scan the QR code to take the quiz on the section 'Amazing Facts''

CODE-Gm8F

43 World of Records

Dog lover **Mitchell Rudy (Canada)** took a 38-strong pack of pooches for walkies to break the record for **most dogs walked simultaneously by an individual**.

16-year-old **Eric Kilburn Jr. from Goodrich, Michigan, USA**, has secured a coveted spot in the *Guinness World Records 2025* book for two remarkable achievements.He holds the record for the **largest feet on a living teenager**, with his feet measuring an impressive 34.30 cm (13.50 inches).

In November of 2023, **Pratyaksh Vijay** secured his dream job despite being only 5 years 337 days old.The young boy from India was verified as the **world's youngest yoga instructor (male)** after completing the 200 Hour Yoga Teacher Training Course.

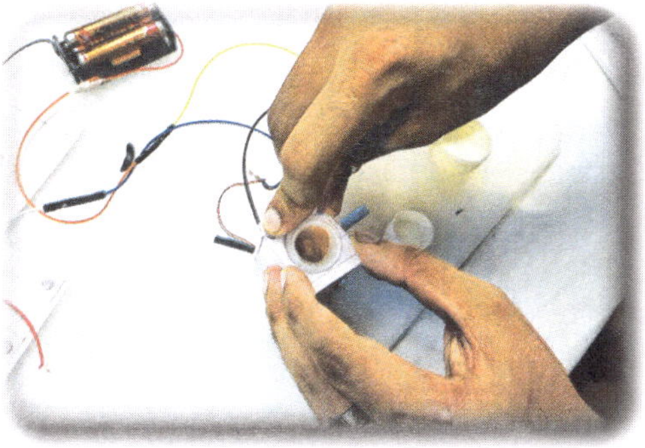

World's smallest washing machine was unveiled in India is tinier than a Tamagotchi. Created by **Sebin Saji**, it measures a teeny tiny 32.5 x 33.6 x 38.7 mm (1.28 x 1.32 x 1.52 in). His little appliance, that he unveiled in Kanjirapally, Kerala, India, on 19 April weighs just 25 g, which is just slightly heavier than two OREO cookies.

During 2024 National Day celebrations, tech took centre stage across China. A massive fleet of **10,200 drones** lit up the night sky, creating a "cyber firework" spectacle that earned drone light show company Damoda not one but two Guinness World Records titles: the **most multirotors/drones airborne simultaneously from a single computer (outdoors)** and the **largest aerial image formed by multirotors/drones**.

A skilled cyclist broke a record by keeping his front wheel off the ground for more than double the length of Hoover Dam. **Dawid Piwowarczyk (Poland)** performed the longest bicycle manual at an incredible distance of 823.60 m (2,702 ft) in Kraków, Poland, on 25 July.

Two co-living properties of a global hospitality brand opened in the Philippines marked their first anniversary with two amazing origami records. The first is the **largest display of origami sharks**, set by **lyf Cebu City**; the other is the **largest display of origami stars**, set by **lyf Malate Manila**.

AI Powered QUIZZES

SECTION QUIZ

Scan the QR code to take the quiz on the section 'Incredible Achievements'

CODE-vENU

Check Point Test-2

(Based on pages 43 to 66)

A. Give your answer in one word.

1. What is *tadasana* posture called in English? ____________
2. What is a group of birds called? ____________
3. Which country does the musical instrument Shamisen come from? ____________
4. Which sport is carried out in a rink? ____________
5. Who invented the radio? ____________

B. Write two examples of each.

1. Religous books ____________ ____________
2. Musical Instruments ____________ ____________
3. Yogaasanas ____________ ____________
4. Emotions ____________ ____________
5. Musical instruments ____________ ____________

C. Tick (✓) the correct choice.

1. Which planet is called the Red planet?

   ◯ Jupiter ◯ Saturn ◯ Mars

2. Which sport is played in a ring?

   ◯ Hockey ◯ Golf ◯ Boxing

3. Which of the following taste food with their feet?

   ◯ Crabs ◯ Cat ◯ Dog

4. Name the planet farthest from the sun.

   ◯ Mars ◯ Jupiter ◯ Neptune

5. Which posture in yoga is the lion posture?

   ◯ *Simhasana* ◯ *Dhyana* ◯ *Katichakrasana*

D. **Identify the following.**

1. ____________ 2. ____________ 3. ____________

4. ____________ 5. ____________ 6. ____________

E. **Write 'T' for True and 'F' for False.**

1. A group of cards is called a pack.
2. Bagpipe is a musical instrument from Scotland.
3. Golf is played in a rink.
4. India won the 2024 ICC Men's T20 World Cup.
5. Cricket is played on a pitch.

F. **Fill in the blanks.**

1. Wind gong is a musical instrument played in the ____________.
2. Kite flying is a professional sport in ____________.
3. Recycle Bin is an icon seen on a ____________.
4. The planet ____________ is named after the speedy messenger of Gods.
5. ____________ is called the father of computer.

44 I.Q. Challenge 3

Tick (✓) the correct answer in each case.

1. 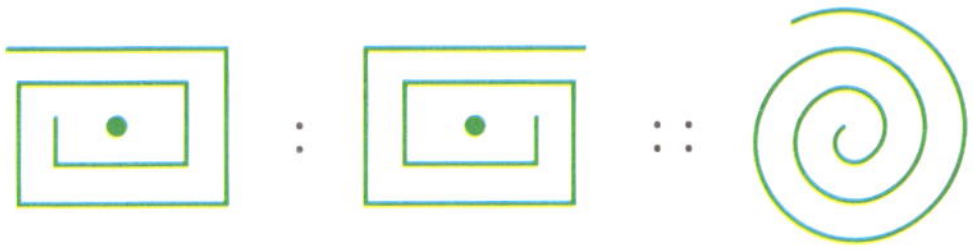 : ?

☐ (a)  ☐ (b)  ☐ (c)  ☐ (d) 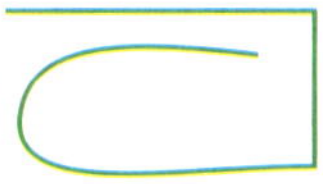

2. 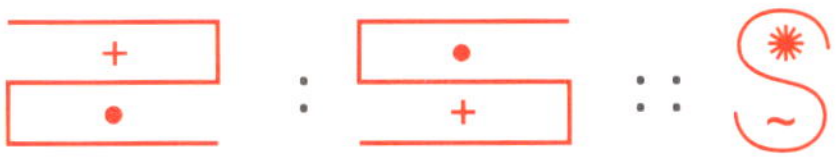 : ?

☐ (a)  ☐ (b)  ☐ (c)  ☐ (d) 

3. How many squares are there in the given figure? 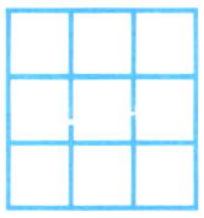

☐ (a) 14 ☐ (b) 13

☐ (c) 12 ☐ (d) 15

4. How many triangles are there in the given figure? 

☐ (a) 10 ☐ (b) 9

☐ (c) 8 ☐ (d) 4

5. The greatest 3-digit number using the digits 2, 5 and 8 only once is:

☐ (a) 258 ☐ (b) 528 ☐ (c) 285 ☐ (d) 852

6. How many rounds does the hour-hand complete in a day?

☐ (a) 1 ☐ (b) 2 ☐ (c) 3 ☐ (d) 4

7. It has 4 sides, 4 corners and all the sides are equal. It is a:

☐ (a) sphere ☐ (b) triangle ☐ (c) rectangle ☐ (d) square

45 Quiz 2

Tick (✓) the correct answer in each case.

1. What is the sport ground of golf called?

   (a) Ring (b) Court (c) Course

2. In which sport do we roll balls to knock down the 10 pins?

   (a) Badminton (b) Bowling (c) Polo

3. Dhyanchand was the famous Indian player of which of the following games?

   (a) Volleyball (b) Football (c) Hockey

4. With which game is the term 'silly point' associated with?

   (a) Chess (b) Golf (c) Cricket

5. Where is the Eden Gardens stadium located?

   (a) Kolkata (b) Mumbai (c) Chennai

6. Which is the top grade in Judo?

   (a) 9th Dan (b) 10th Dan (c) 12th Dan

7. Which among the following is not a grand slam title?

   (a) US Open (b) French Open (c) German Open

8. Who among the following scored 264 runs against Sri Lanka in 2014 in a One-Day International cricket match?

   (a) Virat Kohli (b) Rohit Sharma (c) Virender Sehwag

9. Basketball is the national game of which of these countries?

   (a) USA (b) Russia (c) China

10. Which is the national game of New Zealand?

    (a) Rugby (b) Carrom (c) Judo

Answers

Pages										
4 -5 :	1. (d)	2. (b)	3. (b)	4. (a)	5. (c)	6. (b)	7. (a)	8. (a)	9. (c)	10. (b)
	11. (a)	12. (b)	13. (b)	14. (b)	15. (b)	16. (b)	17. (b)	18. (c)	19. (b)	20. (c)
6 :	1. (e)	2. (d)	3. (c)	4. (f)	5. (g)	6. (b)	7. (h)	8. (a)		
8-9 :	1. (a)	2. (e)	3. (i)	4. (b)	5. (f)	6. (j)	7. (c)	8. (g)	9. (k)	10. (d)
	11. (h)	12 (l)								
11 :	1. (b)	2. (b)	3. (d)	4. (b)	5. (b)	6. (b)	7. (a)	8. (b)	9. (c)	
15 :	1. (b)	2. (c)	3. (c)	4. (a)	5. (a)	6. (a)	7. (b)	8. (c)	9. (a)	
16-17 :	1. (d)	2. (f)	3. (e)	4. (c)	5. (b)	6. (a)	7. (g)	8. (i)	9. (h)	10. (k)
	11. (l)	12 (j)	13. (o)	14. (n)	15. (m)					
18 :	1. (f)	2. (d)	3. (g)	4. (h)	5. (i)	6. (j)	7. (a)	8. (c)	9. (b)	10. (e)
19 :	1. (g)	2. (f)	3. (h)	4. (e)	5. (i)	6. (d)	7. (j)	8. (c)	9. (k)	10. (b)
	11. (l)	12. (a)								
20 :	1. (e)	2. (a)	3. (f)	4. (c)	5. (d)	6. (b)				
21 :	1. (L)	2. (W)	3. (W)	4. (W)	5. (A)	6. (L)	7. (L)	8. (A)	9. (A), (W)	10. (W)
	11. (A)	12. (A)								
22-23 :	For Students									
24 :	Biodegradable : 2, 4, 5, 6, 7, 11									
	Non-Biodegradable : 1, 3, 8, 9, 10, 12									
25 :	1. (i)	2. (d)	3. (e)	4. (a)	5. (b)	6. (h)	7. (f)	8. (c)	9. (g)	
26-27 :	1. (g)	2. (e)	3. (f)	4. (d)	5. (b)	6. (c)	7. (a)			
28-29 :	1. (f)	2. (e)	3. (d)	4. (a)	5. (b)	6. (c)				
30-31 :	For Students									
33 :	1. (c)	2. (b)	3. (d)	4. (h)	5. (i)	6. (f)	7. (g)	8. (e)	9. (a)	10. (j)
34 :	1. Fire station		2. Police station		3. Post Office		4. Hospital	5. School	6. Park	
35-36 :	1. (e)	2. (f)	3. (g)	4. (a), (b)	5. (c)	6. (d)				
37 :	For Students									
40 :	1. (b)	2. (b)	3. (c)	4. (b)						
41 :	1. (b)	2. (c)	3. (b)	4. (d)	5. (c)					
42 :	1. (a)	2. (c)	3. (b)	4. (b)	5. (a)	6. (b)	7. (a)	8. (b)	9. (c)	10. (a)
44-45 :	For Students									
48 :	1. (l)	2. (a)	3. (k)	4. (b)	5. (j)	6. (c)	7. (i)	8. (d)	9. (e)	10. (h)
	11. (f)	12. (g)								
49 :	1. (e)	2. (f)	3. (c)	4. (a)	5. (h)	6. (i)	7. (j)	8. (g)	9. (d)	10. (b)
50 :	1. (c)	2. (d)	3. (b)	4. (g)	5. (i)	6. (f)	7. (k)	8. (l)	9. (h)	10. (a)
	11. (e)	12. (j)								
51 :	1. (g)	2. (e)	3. (l)	4. (o)	5. (m)	6. (h)	7. (d)	8. (f)	9. (i)	10. (j)
	11. (a)	12. (c)	13. (b)	14. (n)	15. (k)					
52 :	1. (k)	2. (a)	3. (j)	4. (b)	5. (i)	6. (c)	7. (h)	8. (d)	9. (g)	10. (e)
	11. (f)	12. (m)	13. (l)							
53-54 :	1. (f)	2. (g)	3. (e)	4. (h)	5. (i)	6. (j)	7. (k)	8. (o)	9. (l)	10. (m)
	11. (n)	12. (a)	13. (b)	14. (c)	15. (d)					

56	:	1. (b)	2. (b)	3. (b)	4. (a)					
57	:	1. (e)	2. (c)	3. (h)	4. (d)	5. (b)	6. (a)	7. (f)	8. (g)	
58-59	:	1. (h)	2. (g)	3. (f)	4. (e)	5. (i)	6. (d)	7. (c)	8. (b)	9. (a)
60-61	:	1. Mercury	2. Venus	3. Earth	4. Mars	5. Jupiter	6. Uranus	7. Neptune	8. Saturn	
62	:	1. (d)	2. (h)	3. (f)	4. (c)	5. (a)	6. (g)	7. (i)	8. (b)	9. (e)
69	:	1. (c)	2. (b)	3. (a)	4. (c)	5. (d)	6. (b)	7. (d)		
70	:	1. (c)	2. (b)	3. (c)	4. (c)	5. (a)	6. (c)	7. (c)	8. (b)	9. (a) 10. (a)

Check Point Test-1

A. : 1. Gujarat 2. *Pookolam* 3. Peacock 4. Telangana 5. Pacific Ocean

B. For students

C. : 1. Berry 2. Italy 3. New Zealand 4. Life 5. Peregrine falcon

D. : 1. Mohiniattam 2. Chaowkpurana 3. Red Panda 4. Taj Mahal 5. The Sphinx 6. Guinea pig

E. : 1. T 2. T 3. F 4. F 5. T

F. : 1. *Avial* 2. Atlantic 3. Banyan 4. Egypt 5. Jellyfish

Check Point Test-2

A. : 1. Palm tree posture 2. Flock 3. Japan 4. Skating 5. Marconi

B. For Students

C. : 1. Mars 2. Boxing 3. Crabs 4. Neptune 5. *Simhasana*

D. : 1. *Simhasana* 2. Microsoft Edge 3. Tar from Iran 4. Magpie 5. Court 6. Rubab

E. : 1. T 2. T 3. F 4. T 5. T

F. : 1. Philippines 2. Thailand 3. Computer screen 4. Mercury 5. Charles Babbage

Disclaimer

QR Codes in this book provide access to AI-generated content, information, quizzes, and interactions from external sources. This material is not created by the publisher and has been included solely to support learning. Readers are advised to verify this information independently. The publisher is not responsible for any consequences arising from its use.

GOYAL BROTHERS PRAKASHAN
EDUCATIONAL PUBLISHERS

Sales & Registered Office :
11/1903, Chuna Mandi, Paharganj, New Delhi - 110055
Post Box : 5720, Phones : 43551877 & 43561877

Administrative Office :
D-231, Sector 63, Noida-201301 (U.P.)
Phone : 0120-4655555
Website : www.goyal-books.com
E-mail : info@goyal-books.com

Showrooms :
Ahmedabad : 09925004030
Chennai : 044-22552767
Kolkata : 033-22262683
Hyderabad : 040-23211332
Bengaluru : 080-23320655
Guwahati : 0361-2967044
Lucknow : 0522-2320841
Nagpur : 9823655077
Bhopal : 0755-4271371
Kochi : 0484-2305288
Patna : 0612-2521030